DATE DUE

The
Sleepy Baker

A Collection of Stories and Recipes for Children

■ ■ ■

Inspired by a Childhood in Norway,
with Monthly Glimpses into the Lives
of Scandinavian Children

by Christin Fjeld Drake
illustrated by Alexandra Eldridge

Northland Publishing

For all my children.
Special thanks to Karen Bannon
for all your help
—C.D.

For my sons,
Saxon and Sebastian.
—A.E.

FIRST EDITION

ISBN 0-87358-551-8
Library of Congress Catalog Card Number 92-56509
Cataloging-in-Publication Data
Drake, Christin.
The sleepy baker : a collection of stories and recipes for children /
by Christin Fjeld Drake ; illustrated by Alexandra Eldridge.
56 p.
Summary: Includes twelve original stories, inspired by the author's
childhood in Norway and peopled by kings, beggars, trolls, dragons,
witches, and clever children, and each accompanied by a recipe.
ISBN 0-87358-551-8 : $14.95
1. Children's stories, American. [1. Cookery—Fiction. 2. Short
stories.] I. Eldridge, Alexandra, 1948- ill. II. Title.
PZ7.D782445S1 1993
[Fic]—dc20   92-56509

Book Design by Larry Lindahl

Manufactured in Hong Kong by Colorcorp, Inc.

4-93/5M/0417

Contents

July
THE SLEEPY BAKER

Pepper Cookies

27

August
THE HUNGRY DRAGON

Norwegian Pancakes

31

September
BEFRIENDING THE TROLLS

Troll Chicken

35

October
THE NASTY WITCH

Magician's Brew

39

November
THE BIG PURPLE SPIDER

Bug Cupcakes

43

December
THE NISSE'S CHRISTMAS

Jule Porridge

47

Before You Begin

Make sure you have everything you need.

✤

Wash your hands and always remember to clean up after yourself.

✤

Make sure that you measure things correctly.
If you don't, the food you are making will not turn out the way it should.

✤

When you measure with a cup or a spoon, don't heap it; level it off at the top.

✤

Always have a grown-up help you in the kitchen.

The Snow Cone King

T HERE WAS ONCE a kind and wise king who was always trying to think of new ways to make the lives of the people in his kingdom better. Winter had come early one year, and some of the harvest had frozen before it could be saved. The people would not go hungry, but neither would they have any extra.

One evening, the king took a walk through the village. It was very cold, and with every step he made, the dry, white snow made a crunching sound under his heavy boots.

"If we could only eat snow," the king said to himself. "No one would ever be hungry."

The king had never cooked anything and he did not know how food was put together. "Maybe, if I brought some snow home and gave it to the cook, he could come up with something," thought the king.

The king entered the castle kitchen with an armful of snow. "Make something edible out of this snow," he ordered the cook, then turned and left.

The cook was distraught. "The king has lost his mind!" he said to the kitchen boy. "Everybody knows that snow only melts and what you get is water."

But since the king had ordered him to try, try he did. The cook added snow to the fried fish; it only made the fish soggy. He added snow to the Sunday roast, but it only made more drippings for gravy. Then he added snow to the cake batter. It made it too thin and the cake came out flat.

"I give up!" the cook said to the kitchen boy. "Snow can only make water and that's it!"

"Sometimes," the boy said, "I like to eat snow. Maybe if you add a little raspberry or blueberry syrup to the snow, stir it a little and then eat it right away, it could be good."

"Yes! You're right!" the cook said happily. "That could be done."

The cook and the boy spent the rest of the afternoon experimenting and eating snow ices. When the cook presented the new invention to the king, he was not very happy. However, the king understood that in order to turn snow into food he needed a magician and not a cook, but that's another story. At least the village children enjoyed the newly invented treat, for the main ingredient was plentiful all winter long. After that day, their king had a new name: The Snow Cone King.

January days in Scandinavia are very short and somewhat dark because the sun never rises above the edge of the horizon. Children amuse themselves during the long month by building snow castles that they decorate with lit candles left over from Christmas.

Snow Cones
— SERVES 6 —

YOU WILL NEED: 2 bowls for mixing, 1 whisk

6 cups of snow
1 cup cranberry juice or jelly
½ cup sugar

1. Use only fresh, clean snow. Collect 6 cups of snow and place it in a mixing bowl. Leave it outside until you are ready.

2. Pour the cranberry juice* or jelly into a separate bowl and mix in the sugar. Get the snow from outside and whisk everything together quickly.

3. Put flavored snow in cups and eat.

You can use just about any juice you like: raspberry, blackberry, pineapple, and orange juices are good.

Beggar's Magic

O N A SUNNY AFTERNOON, a poor beggar walked into the village square. The woman who sold vegetables out of a cart turned to her customer and said, "Beggars. They're all alike. They take and never give!"

The beggar overheard what was being said and replied, "I never beg. I can make magic. I can make things happen."

"Oh," said the woman, "show us then."

The beggar dug his hands deep in his pocket and pulled out a nail. "I can make a delicious soup out of this nail," he claimed. He made a fire on the ground and pulled from his bag a pot, filled it with water, and put it on the fire. He dropped the nail into the water.

The beggar sat down next to the pot and said, "I'm waiting for the water to boil, then you will see that this will be the best soup you have ever tasted. The only thing that would make this soup better is if I had an onion to add to the soup."

"I have an onion for you," volunteered the old lady in the green shawl. The beggar took the onion, and with a small knife, peeled it and cut it into small pieces, then dropped it into the soup.

After a short while, the beggar muttered to himself, "This soup would be even better if I had a meat bone to put in it."

"Well," exclaimed the man in the yellow rain slicker, "it so happens that I have an extra meat bone." He dropped the bone into the soup. A short while later, the soup started to smell very good.

"Here are four carrots," a little boy piped up. "I grew them myself. You can have them for your soup."

"Thanks," the beggar said. He cleaned and peeled the carrots carefully, chopped them up, and dropped them into the soup.

"The soup may be good," said an old man sitting on a rock close by, "but I have never tasted a good soup without a few potatoes. Look here," he continued, "they are cleaned, peeled, and cut up. Just throw them into your pot of soup." The soup went on simmering over the fire. Everyone looked on, getting hungrier by the minute.

"Well," the beggar told them, "the soup should be done in a few hours."

"A few hours!" the people echoed. "We are hungry now."

"The only things that can hurry the soup," the beggar said, "would be a little salt, pepper, and maybe some chopped celery."

"I have that," a farm woman told the crowd. "You can have it so the soup will be done and we will not have to wait so long." The beggar cleaned and cut the celery into little pieces and added it, along with the salt and pepper, to the soup. It didn't take long for the soup to be done. The beggar filled everyone's cup with the delicious soup.

"Isn't it wonderful?" the woman with the vegetable cart declared. "A soup made with only a nail!"

On the 8th of February, the people in the town of Narvik, in the far north of Norway, celebrate the return of the sun, which has been absent for many months. This is a magic day that is celebrated with parades, hot food, and dancing in the streets.

Nail Soup
— SERVES 6 —

YOU WILL NEED: a knife, a cutting board, a soup pot

6 cups of water
4 carrots
1 onion
4 potatoes
1 large soup bone
   (with some meat on it)

5 stalks of celery
1 teaspoon salt
¼ teaspoon pepper
3 teaspoons beef bouillon,
   if the soup doesn't
   taste strong enough

1. Pour the water in the pot.

2. Peel and clean the carrots, cut them up into small pieces, and put them in the pot. Do the same with the onion and the potatoes.

3. Add the bone to the water. Clean the stalks of celery, cut them into small pieces, and add them to the water. Add salt and pepper.

4. Let the soup simmer* for 1 hour. Add beef stock, if you need it.

*Simmer: To cook on very low heat.

Naming Astrid

THE BOY SAT QUIETLY next to the cradle. His baby sister had been born earlier that evening, and his mother had asked him to give the baby a name. He had been named after the god Thor, who represents strength and luck.

Thor could not sleep. To be asked to give a name was a serious request. After all, the name he chose would be with his sister her entire life. It would help define who she would become and how people would respond to her. He looked at the beautiful new baby as she lay sleeping peacefully, swaddled in a blanket. He looked at her for some sign, for some clue about what her name should be. It was difficult for him to think of an appropriate name.

The spring night was still. Not a leaf nor a flower stirred. It was as if everything was waiting for Thor to name the baby. He thought for what seemed like hours, but no name came to him.

Thor looked up into the dark night sky. Every star was bright, and he remembered what his grandma had told him.

"If you can't think of a name," she had said, "take my apron and spread it out on top of the hill. By sunrise, a star will fall into it. Take that star into your hands and a name will come to you. That name will be the right one. That name will bring more light days than dark into the child's life."

So, Thor took his grandma's apron and went outside. He climbed to the top of the grassy hill, unfolded the apron, and draped it across the land. He paused for a moment to feel the cool, crisp air and to notice how the starlight cast its shadows upon the earth. Then, he went back inside to sit by the cradle. Soon, he too was fast asleep.

When he awakened to the first rays of sun shining through the window, he went outside and up the hill to see if a star had fallen. Indeed, just as his grandma had predicted, he found a tiny star on the apron. As he picked up the star, Thor thought, "Astrid must be her name. My baby sister must indeed be blessed, for Astrid means 'star' in the old language. Not only have the stars named her, they have named her after themselves."

Thor returned to the house bursting with excitement, for now he had a name for his sister. Everyone was delighted with the name and agreed that it fit the child perfectly, for she became a bright, beautiful, and loving little girl, full of heavenly grace. And Thor was, indeed, very proud to have played such an important role in giving her a name.

So, from that day until this, it has become customary to serve star cookies with names written on them to celebrate new births and birthdays.

The first Sunday in March is the last day before Lent. Children pick branches from birch trees and decorate them with feathers. They use them to tickle and spank their parents, and demand that they make cream puffs for breakfast. Children are spoiled on this day because they are allowed no luxuries during Lent.

Star Cookies
— MAKES 3 DOZEN —

YOU WILL NEED: a mixing bowl, a rolling pin, star-shaped cookie cutters, cookie trays

1 cup sugar
½ cup butter
2 cups flour
¼ teaspoon nutmeg
1 teaspoon baking
   powder
1 egg

1 teaspoon vanilla or
   almond extract
1 egg white for glazing

ICING:
2 ¼ cups powdered sugar
1 teaspoon cream of tartar
2 egg whites

1. In a bowl, beat (mix well together with a wooden spoon or electric beater) the sugar and butter until it is fluffy and lighter in color.

2. Add all other dry ingredients to the butter-and-sugar mixture and beat some more.

3. Add the egg and vanilla, making sure to mix well.

4. Put the dough in the refrigerator for 1 hour or more.

5. Heat the oven to 350 degrees.

6. Sprinkle a little flour on the table and roll out the cookie dough until it is about ⅛ inch thick (or pretty thin).

7. Use star-shaped cookie cutters to cut out the dough. Then put the stars on a lightly greased cookie tray or waxed paper.

8. Use a pastry brush to brush some egg white on top of each cookie. Bake the cookies for about 10 minutes, or until golden yellow.

ICING:

1. Beat all ingredients together until smooth.

2. Use a pastry tube* to frost the edges of the cookies or spread the icing on top of the cookies with a butter knife.

*Pastry tube: A cone made of plastic or cloth with a little piece at the end to squeeze cream or icing out. You can make your own pastry tube by cutting a hole in one corner of a plastic sandwich bag. After you have filled the pastry tube, make sure to hold it together at the top so the icing doesn't come out the wrong way.

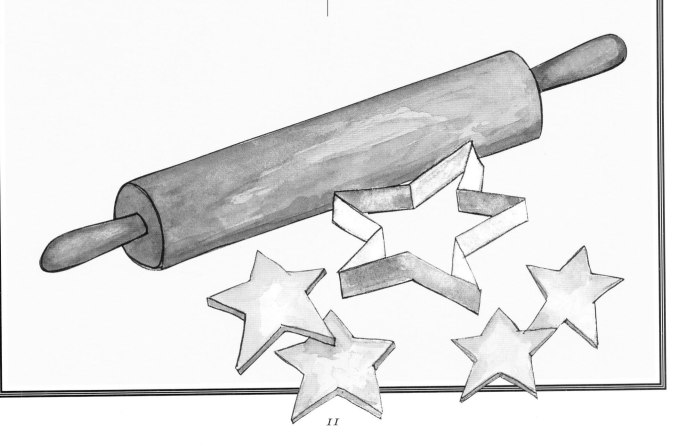

A Day with the Easter Rabbits

I T WAS EARLY SPRING, just before Easter. The little boy ran as fast as he could up the driveway. He stumbled up the stairs and threw the door open.

"I saw them!" he yelled to his mother and brother. "I told you they were real. They had big ears. The little one was just a little big and the big one a little small, so really, they were almost the same size."

"Björn," Mother said. "Slow down. You are not making any sense."

"But it's true," he told her. "They are for real."

"Who?" asked his brother, Alf. "Who is real?"

"The Easter rabbits, of course," Björn whispered. "I saw them in a meadow. They were painting Easter eggs."

"Enough of this nonsense," Mother exclaimed. "Wash your hands. It's almost time for dinner."

"Do you believe me, Alf?" Björn asked, as the boys washed their hands.

"I don't know," Alf answered. "Why don't you show them to me tomorrow?"

Björn could hardly sleep a wink that night. With the first light of morning, he got up, went into his brother's room, and shook him awake.

"Come on. Let's go," Björn whispered.

"Okay, okay," Alf replied. "Just let me put on some clothes and shoes."

The meadow Björn had talked about was not far from their home.

"Hush!" murmured Björn. "We will wait here. The rabbits might be scared if they see us."

The two boys crept under a bush to wait quietly for the rabbits. All of a sudden, someone yelled into their ears.

"Boo!"

Björn and Alf got such a fright they both fell over.

"I scared you, didn't I?" chortled the little rabbit, as he rolled on the ground, giggling.

"Yes, you did," said Alf. "That's not very nice."

"Maybe not," the little brown rabbit replied, "but I didn't mean to scare you that much. Have you had breakfast yet?" he asked. "Come and have some breakfast with me."

The boys didn't need to be asked twice. They followed the little brown rabbit to a big willow tree at the edge of the meadow.

The little brown rabbit disappeared into a small hole under the tree. He was soon back with a teapot filled with steaming hot dandelion tea. His mother, father, four sisters, and two brothers came out bearing Easter bread, honey, butter, and a big basket of painted Easter eggs.

They all settled down in the grass to have breakfast.

The Easter bread was a braided piece of bread that had been baked with a red egg in the middle. It was soft and sweet.

Björn made a funny face as he tasted the tea.

"It's bitter, isn't it?" said the little brown rabbit. "Put heaps of honey in it like I do."

Björn and Alf had a good time with their new friends. Now they knew that Easter rabbits really existed.

"Back to work," the papa rabbit announced. "We have much to do before Easter Sunday."

"Can we help?" Alf asked.

"Of course," answered the papa rabbit. "We can use all the help we can get."

The boys helped paint Easter eggs and fill pink, green, yellow, and white baskets with goodies. It was fun, and they learned how to cook and dye eggs using onion peel and flowers for coloring.

Björn and Alf also learned how to make the rabbits' Easter bread. They decided to make this at home for their parents for Easter breakfast.

Around noon, the boys left, for rabbits take long naps in the middle of the day.

After Björn and Alf had returned home, they told their mother where they had been and about the Easter rabbits. They could tell from the look on her face that she was not convinced.

"You will see," Björn said, "when we make this special Easter bread."

"Oh, really?" Mother asked, disbelievingly.

As you can imagine, their mother was very surprised when she awoke on Easter morning to the smell of freshly baked Easter bread and steaming dandelion tea. From that day on, and until the boys grew up, they always helped the rabbits with Easter preparations.

Easter Bread

YOU WILL NEED: a small saucepan, a large bowl, a baking tray

¼ pound butter	1 teaspoon salt
3 cups milk	½ cup sugar
2 packages yeast	1 egg white for glaze
1 egg	3 eggs hardboiled and dyed
6 cups flour	with food coloring

1. Put the butter and milk in the saucepan. Melt the butter in the milk over low heat. Turn off the heat and let the mixture cool until you can dip your finger into it. Stir in the yeast, let sit for 5 minutes, add the egg, and mix.

2. Pour the flour, salt and sugar into the large bowl and combine. Then pour the yeast, milk, and egg into the flour mixture.

3. Using your hands, knead* it all together for about 5 minutes. Then cover the bowl with a tea towel and set it in a warm place to rise for 45 minutes.

4. Take the risen dough out of the bowl and knead it again, adding a little more flour, for about 10 minutes.

5. Divide the dough into 3 equal balls. Divide each ball into 3 pieces. Roll out each piece to look like a snake. Take 3 snakes and braid (or twist) them together.

6. Now you should have 3 braids. Form each braid into a circle and place it on the cookie tray. Make sure they are not too close together. Put a colored egg in the middle of the braid.

7. Brush the bread braid with egg white.

8. Set the bread in a warm place for about 1 hour or until the bread is almost twice the size it was before.

9. Heat the oven to 350 degrees. When the oven is hot, put the bread into it and bake for about 20 minutes.

Knead: Squeeze the dough with both of your hands and push it down again with the heels of your hands, then gather the dough together and do it again.

The Flower Fairy

I T WAS DARK OUTSIDE, and the moon shone its light on the little girl and her grandmother as they sat on the bed.

"Tell me of the flower fairy again," the little girl requested.

"That I will," the grandmother said, and she started her story.

"The first time I saw the fairy, I was your age. She was sitting on my bedroom windowsill, and the moonlight made everything seem so unreal, just like tonight. The fairy had shiny, dark hair. She was very small and was dressed in a sparkling blue dress. Her wings were shimmering silver and translucent (which means you could see through them). I wanted to get up out of bed and get a closer look, but I thought I might scare her away.

"As I was thinking these thoughts, she turned her head and looked straight at me. Then, she was gone.

"The next time I saw her was after my grandfather's funeral. Everything in the house was so sad, and all the rooms in the house were filled with the strong smell of dead flowers. I opened my bedroom window and climbed over the sill to sit in the garden. The grass smelled so fresh and alive. It was May, my favorite month of them all.

"That's when I saw her for the second time. She was flying slowly through the apple trees, sprinkling tiny stars with her wand.

" 'What are you doing?' I whispered. 'Can you tell me?'

"To my big surprise, she flew straight to me, sat down on my knee, and rested her head in one hand.

"In a tiny voice, she told me, 'I am a flower fairy, and I help to wake up the flowers and all things growing. Without us flower fairies, the flowers might forget to wake up at all and sleep until next spring. You watch, in just a week, you will see all sorts of wonderful things growing in your garden. Maybe when the raspberries are ripe, you can make me some raspberry jam, for that is my favorite.'

" 'Of course I will,' I promised.

Norway's Independence Day is May 17th. The children dress in their national costumes and participate in the neighborhood parade, in which they wave their flags and shout "Harra for Norge!" ("Hoorah for Norway!"). After the parade they play games and eat hot dogs and ice cream.

" 'I have work to do,' the fairy said. And, in a shower of sparkling stars, she was gone.

"I could hardly wait for the berries to ripen, especially the raspberries, for it took all summer.

"First, the bushes sprouted new, light green leaves. Then, the flowers opened up with a show of pretty, white blossoms. In another week, the petals of the blossoms fell off and tiny, hard, green knobs formed instead. Slowly, slowly, the green knobs turned to dark red, berries.

"I saw the fairy a few times that summer, especially on warm summer afternoons when no one else was around. Sometimes she would come and sit on my hand and talk to me in her funny, tiny voice about all the things that lived in the garden, big and small.

"Late in the summer, when many of the raspberry bushes had ripe berries, I picked a whole bucketful. My father showed me how to make jam. It was not difficult. Unfortunately, I burned my hand quite badly by spilling hot jam on it. My father had to finish filling all the jars with jam.

"I picked out a pretty jar and on the label I wrote, 'To my favorite fairy: Enjoy this jam. Love, Me.'

"That night, I put the jar of jam on my bedroom windowsill and sat down to wait. It wasn't difficult to stay awake for my hand still stung from the burn.

"It was almost midnight when the fairy came. She was so delighted with the jam that she made a merry dance around the jar. Then she whistled, and out of nowhere came at least a dozen other fairies. They had a net to carry the jam. I put the jar of jam in the net and they flew off with it. My fairy stayed behind.

"She put her tiny hands on my burn, and to my surprise, the pain was gone.

" 'Now open your hands,' she said, 'and close your eyes.'

"I did as she told me and when I opened my eyes the fairy was gone. But, in my hand, was the most beautiful flower-shaped crystal. It was pale pink and sparkled. Later, I had it made into a necklace that I wear always."

"Can I see the necklace?" the girl asked.

The grandmother took off the necklace and put it around the girl's neck.

"From now on, the necklace is yours. May it bring you the luck it has always brought me."

The grandmother kissed the girl goodnight.

The girl said, "Goodnight, Grandma. I love you." She turned over in bed so that she could see the window better. There, on the ledge, sat a tiny fairy eating raspberry jam out of an itsy, bitsy silver bowl.

"You know," the fairy said, "raspberry jam tastes great in a truffle."

Raspberry Jam
— MAKES 3 CUPS —

YOU WILL NEED: a large saucepan, a wooden spoon, jars with lids to store the jam

    6 cups raspberries
    2 cups sugar
    2 teaspoons of lemon juice

1. Clean and rinse the raspberries and put them in the pot with the sugar and lemon juice. Let them simmer on low heat for about 45 minutes but stir once in a while to prevent them from sticking to the pan.

2. Let the raspberry jam cool before you pour it into the jars.

3. This jam will keep for about 3 weeks in the refrigerator or one year if you freeze it.

Cecilia Lind's Bad Day

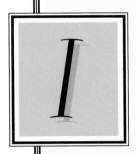

I WAS ANGRY and upset. I, Cecilia Lind, had been grounded to my room for the whole day and was allowed downstairs only for meals. I knew it had been wrong to let the birds out of the cage, but they looked so sad locked up. Birds are meant to fly, aren't they?

After setting the birds free, I had gone down the road to my friend's house. She was not there, but on the way back to my house, I found a tiny, cute, white kitten. It fit right into the pocket of my dress. I knew my mom would not let me keep it, so I hid it in the pantry. How was I to know that she had just finished my brother's birthday cake?

The cake had been made with peaches and cream and placed on the bottom shelf in the pantry. When my mother opened the pantry door, we saw what had happened. The kitten must have really liked cream because it had licked off all the cream and made tiny little pawprints in the cake.

"We can still eat it," I tried to convince my mother, but she would not listen.

"To your room, Cecilia Lind. I am very angry!" she said. "First, you let the canaries out and then, you put a stray cat into the pantry!"

I knew better than to argue with her so, sadly, I went up to my room.

As I sat in my room, I tried to think of something that would make everyone happy again. My brother's birthday party was that evening and I did not want to miss it. What would you do if you were me? I thought perhaps I could make my brother a new birthday cake.

I remembered that Grandma was coming this afternoon to watch my brother and me while my parents picked up his present in town. I knew I could count on Grandma to help me make a new cake because she understood me better than anyone else. I quickly counted how much I had in my piggy bank.

"Three dollars and fifteen cents," I thought. "That should be enough."

I waited until I saw my mom and dad drive away before I ran downstairs to tell Grandma of my plan. Grandma not only said she would help me but she also said that

I should go down to Olsen's farm and pick some strawberries for the cake. I grabbed my basket and the money for the strawberries and ran.

Mr. Olsen said that it would be okay to eat a few berries while I filled my basket. They were red, sweet, and delicious.

When my basket was full, Mr. Olsen said, "That's only a dollar's worth."

Because I had money left, I decided to stop at the toy store to buy a little fire engine for my brother. Fire engines were among his favorite things.

At home, Grandma had everything ready for the cake. I put on an apron and washed my hands and we got busy.

By the time my parents got back, we had the cake baked, the kitchen cleaned up, and the fire engine wrapped. Grandma, by the way, thought that the kitten was cute and agreed to take it home.

It was great to have a grandma who thought like I did—almost. She said that she would not have let the birds out because they were tropical birds and could not survive the winter on their own.

"At least they got a few months of freedom," I said.

My mom was pleased with the cake and said that I did not have to be grounded anymore. She also said, "You need to think about what you do before you do it."

"Okay, Mom," I said. "I promise to think more."

"Your problem," Grandma whispered in my ear, "is that, sometimes, you think too much!"

After the party, when my mom kissed me goodnight, she said, "That was a very good cake you made. It makes me proud to have such a good cook for a daughter."

June 24th in Scandinavia is Midsummer Eve, the longest day of the year. It never gets very dark on this night because the sun only leaves the sky for a couple of hours. Children gather flowers to decorate their homes and wear in their hair. In the evening there are huge bonfires, and people gather to eat, drink, and sing songs until very late.

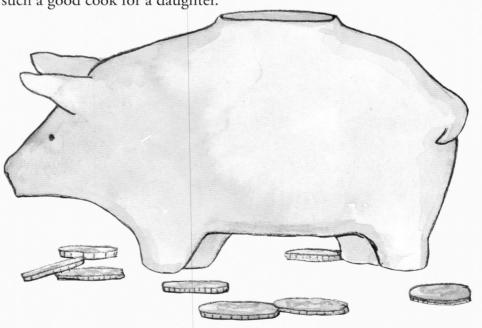

Strawberry Cake

— MAKES 1 CAKE —

YOU WILL NEED: a big mixing bowl, 2 small bowls, a 9" spring form or cake pan

CAKE:
1 teaspoon margarine
1 tablespoon flour
4 tablespoons butter
7 eggs
1 ¼ cups sugar
2 teaspoons vanilla extract

¾ teaspoon cream of tartar
1 ½ cups flour, sifted

FILL AND TOPPING:
2 pints strawberries
1 pint whipping cream
¼ cup sugar

1. Heat oven to 350 degrees.

2. Put a teaspoonful of magarine on a piece of paper towel and smear it around inside of the cake pan. Then, take 1 tablespoonful of flour and shake it around until it completely covers the inside of the pan.

3. In a saucepan, melt the butter, making sure not to let it turn brown.

4. Using 2 small bowls, separate the egg whites from the egg yolks. Put the egg whites in one bowl and the egg yolks in the other.

5. Pour the egg yolks into a big bowl and add the sugar. Beat 5 minutes, then add the vanilla and the melted butter, and beat a little longer.

6. Pour the egg whites into a very clean, dry bowl, add the cream of tartar, then beat the mixture until it stands up by itself in little peaks.

[*continued on page 24*]

7. Combine the flour with the egg-yolk-and-sugar mixture and keep stirring until you can't see the flour any more and it forms a batter.

8. Next, pour the egg white mixture into the flour batter.

9. With a spoon, gently fold* the two batters together. When this is done, and everything is carefully mixed, pour the batter into the cake pan and put it in the heated oven.

10. Bake for 30 minutes, or until the cake is light brown on top. (When you stick a toothpick into the cake, it should come out clean.)

11. While the cake is baking, rinse the strawberries under cold running water. Save the 12 prettiest strawberries for decoration. Snip the stems off the other strawberries and cut each one into 3 slices.

*Fold: Use a metal or plastic spoon. Lift a spoonful of batter from the bottom of the bowl and place it on top of the rest of the batter and carefully repeat until it is all blended together.

12. Pour the whipping cream and sugar into a clean bowl and beat until the cream is stiff. (Be careful not to beat it too long or you will have lumpy butter instead!)

13. When you take the cake out of the oven, let it cool for 15 minutes before you remove it from the cake pan. Use a knife to loosen the cake from the sides of the cake pan.

14. Put the cake on a plate and gently slide a knife sideways through it to cut it in half.

15. Lift the top half off and put it aside. Then, take half of the strawberries you have sliced and cover the bottom half of the cake with the fruit. Next, spread half the whipped cream over the strawberries. Now, put the top of the cake back on.

16. Finish off the cake by covering it with the remaining whipped cream. Using a knife, spread it evenly all over the cake. Finally, decorate the cake with the rest of the strawberries.

July

The Sleepy Baker

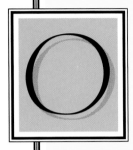

NCE UPON A TIME, there was a sleepy baker. Bakers are often tired because they never have time to sleep. They are up early in the morning baking bread and pastries and they stay up late at night baking cakes and cookies. Then they spend their days selling what they have baked.

The sleepy baker was more than tired; he could barely keep his eyes open. Often, he fell asleep in the middle of his baking, which led to disastrous results. He would then have to start all over again, leaving him with even less time to sleep. But, this was not the baker's biggest problem; the naughty squirrels that lived in a tree outside the bakery were his biggest problem.

While the baker was busy baking or snoozing, these naughty squirrels would sneak into the bakery and steal cookies. Their favorite cookies were the pepper cookies. The baker often found he was completely out of pepper cookies because of the squirrels.

Then one day, a young boy looking for work knocked at the baker's door.

"I want to learn how to bake," he declared.

"Well," said the baker as he watched the squirrels in the tree eating his pepper cookies, "I do the baking but I need someone to chase those naughty, greedy squirrels away and to keep me awake."

"I can do all three!" the boy exclaimed. "I can learn to bake, chase the squirrels away, and keep you awake."

"It is worth a try," the baker agreed. "You can have the job."

So, over the next few weeks, the boy kept very busy baking cakes, chasing squirrels, and waking the baker. But, one day, the baker fell asleep on the bread table. He was so fast asleep that the boy could not wake him.

"Never mind," he thought to himself. "I'll bake the pepper cookies myself and let the baker sleep a while."

While the boy mixed the batter, he threw measuring cups at the squirrels, who were trying any way they could to snatch a few cookies.

Because there were so many recipes to remember, the boy had made up a song for each one. He sang to himself as he got out the pots and pans: "When a baker boy bakes cookies and cakes, the first thing he must remember is to . . ."

He stopped singing. "Was it a quarter cup of pepper or was it a quarter teaspoon?" he asked himself. "It's probably a quarter cup." He added the pepper to the batter.

After mixing the cookie dough, the boy rolled it out with a rolling pin. Then, using cookie cutters, he cut the dough into many different shapes. On a greased cookie tray, he carefully arranged the cut shapes and put the tray in the oven. After a few minutes, the bakery was filled with the wonderful aroma of pepper cookies.

Meanwhile, the squirrels were hiding, waiting for an opportunity to steal the cookies. They got it when the baker rolled over in his sleep and fell face first into the bread dough.

"Help!" the baker hollered. With the help of the boy, the baker finally got out of the bread dough. By that time, the squirrels had made off with every single pepper cookie. There wasn't one left.

Then, something strange happened. A queer noise rose from the squirrels' tree. The baker and the boy looked out the window and saw the squirrels squawk, holler, run across the garden, and dive into the pond.

"What's the matter with those squirrels?" the baker asked. "They're drinking the pond dry!"

The boy did not answer. Now he knew that it was not a quarter cup of pepper, but a quarter teaspoon that was needed to make pepper cookies.

After that day, the boy took over the baking more and more so that the baker could get some rest. The boy soon became a master baker, and to this day, the squirrels have not stolen one single cookie from the bakery. They remain content with the treats the boy sets out for them under the big tree.

Children have no school in the summer, so July is a time of fishing, swimming, camping, biking, and playing ball late into the evenings.

Pepper Cookies
— MAKES 6 DOZEN COOKIES —

YOU WILL NEED: 2 large mixing bowls, 2 cookie trays

1½ cups shortening
1½ cups brown sugar
8 cups flour

1¾ teaspoons cinnamon
2 tablespoons ginger
1½ teaspoons ground cloves

¼ teaspoon pepper
1½ cups dark corn syrup
2¼ teaspoons baking soda
3 eggs

ICING:
1 pound powdered sugar
1 teaspoon cream of tartar
1½ teaspoons lemon juice
2 egg whites

1. Put the shortening in a bowl and stir in the brown sugar. Keep stirring until it is well blended.

2. Next, put aside ½ cup of the flour to prevent the cookie dough from sticking when you roll it out later.

3. Add all other batter ingredients, including the flour, to the sugar-and-shortening mixture. Knead with your hands until it is smooth.

4. Put the dough in a plastic bag and place it in a very cool place or the refrigerator for 3 hours or more.

5. Then, heat the oven to 350 degrees. Take the dough out of the refrigerator and cut it into 4 pieces. Roll out one piece of the dough at a time, using a rolling pin and a little of the flour you have saved. The dough should be about ½ inch thick. Use your favorite cookies cutters to cut out the cookies.

6. Arrange the cookies on a greased cookie tray.

7. Put the tray in the oven for about 7 minutes (check the cookies after 4 or 5 minutes; your oven may cook faster than mine).

8. Remove the cookies from the oven and allow them to cool.

ICING:
1. Pour the powdered sugar into a mixing bowl. Add the cream of tartar and lemon juice.

2. Crack the eggs and separate the egg yolks from the egg whites. Then, pour the egg whites into the powdered sugar and beat for 10 minutes.

3. Add food coloring if you like.

4. Ice the cookies with a pastry tube, or spread the icing on the cookies with a butter knife.

The Hungry Dragon

HE DRAGON had not been out for days. It had been raining and he hated getting wet, but his stomach was growling. So, he went to the far corner of his cave and there, in his treasure chest, among gold coins and jewels, he found his rainboots, an old umbrella, and a bucket for his cloudberries, special berries that grow in Norway.

He ventured outside. Looking up at the clouds and the pouring rain, he grumbled, "It's miserable, but at least there aren't any hunters out in this rain." The dragon was afraid of hunters. Most of the dragons he had known had either been chased, like himself, into small caves high in the mountains or shot dead. There were no berries near the steep cliffs of his cave, so he had to climb down to the valley and up another mountain, where he knew there would be plenty of cloudberries.

After the dragon had filled his bucket with berries, he decided to take a different path home. Maybe he would be lucky enough to find some wild cherries, too.

On the way, the dragon had to pass a lonely cabin. No smoke rose from the chimney, so he presumed that no one lived there anymore. But, as he passed by, he heard people inside. The dragon hurried by.

A child's voice yelled, "Wait! Wait!"

The dragon turned, and there on the path behind him stood a small, scrawny boy with sandy blonde hair. In a cranky voice the dragon asked, "What do you want?"

The dragon looked scary to the boy, and he could not remember what he wanted.

"What?" the dragon repeated, as he blew a puff of smoke out of his nose.

The boy remembered. "Fire," he replied. "That is what we need most. My family and I are cold, and my mother can't light the wood-burning stove without fire. She promised us pancakes if we could find fire."

"Well," the dragon said, puffing more smoke, "fire is my specialty. As everyone knows, the one thing dragons are good at is making huge, billowing fire."

"We only need a small fire," the boy went on. "Come," he said, as he tugged at the dragon's leg.

The dragon followed the boy inside the cabin. His brother and sister weren't sure whether to be scared or surprised by the sight of the dragon.

"He's going to help us start a fire," the boy reassured them.

The dragon walked over to the stove and carefully blew a tiny flame onto the wood. Immediately, a fire was started, and the cabin grew cozy and warm in the rosy light of the fire. The dragon almost hated to leave and go out into the rain again.

"Stay a while, Mr. Dragon," the boy's mother invited. "We are poor people and don't have much to offer, but if you would like to eat pancakes with us, you are welcome."

"Yes, thank you. I would like that," the dragon told her. "But, wait a minute. I have a whole bucket of cloudberries by the door. They would taste mighty good on the pancakes."

The children helped clean the cloudberries then mix them up with a little sugar. The dragon insisted on making the pancakes. He soon had a stack of pancakes that almost reached the ceiling. With a stack like that, there was plenty for everyone.

After finishing his plate of pancakes, the dragon started to tell stories from when he was young, and that was almost six hundred years ago. The children were fascinated with his tales of Vikings and sea monsters.

Later on in the evening, when the dragon bade them farewell, the children begged him to come back soon and tell them more stories. So three days later, when the dragon passed by the cabin again, he brought his treasure chest full of gold and jewels.

"These riches are of no use to me," the dragon confided to them, "but they can make life easier for you."

The dragon stopped by the cabin often to share his stories and have supper with the family. And, as far as I know, he still · lives in his cave high in the mountains.

August is the month for harvesting. Children even get a week off from school—a vacation known as a "potato holiday"— so they can help their families or other farmers harvest vegetables, fruits, and berries. Their help is also needed in the kitchen for storing the harvest as well as making jams, pickles, and juices so that they have enough to last far into the winter months.

Norwegian Pancakes
— MAKES 20 PANCAKES —

YOU WILL NEED: a mixing bowl, a frying pan, a spatula

2¼ cups flour
½ teaspoon salt
3 tablespoons sugar
3 cups milk

1 teaspoon vanilla
¼ teaspoon cardamom
3 eggs
butter or margarine for frying

1. In the bowl, mix flour, salt, and sugar. Add the milk a little at a time while stirring. When you have used all the milk, add the vanilla, cardamom, and eggs. Stir until the batter is even (without lumps).

2. Let the batter sit for 20 minutes. Then warm the frying pan and add a little melted butter or margarine.

3. Pour ¼ cup of batter into the frying pan. Tip the frying pan from side to side to even out the batter.

4. Flip the pancake with a spatula and fry until light brown. Store the pancakes between two plates to keep them warm until you have used up all the batter.

5. Top the pancakes with berries or strawberry jam, sugar and butter, or whatever you prefer.

6. Roll up the pancakes with the toppings inside.

These pancakes are very thin like crepes, not thick like flapjacks.

Befriending the Trolls

HE TROLL MAMA was busy putting all of her eleven troll children to bed. She had almost finished tying their tails together so they would lie still when the littlest troll jumped out of bed and whined, "I don't want to go to sleep. Sleep is so boring. Can't we play just a little longer?"

"Not a chance," said the troll mama. "I am tired."

"Why do we have to sleep when you are tired?" the little troll whined again.

"Because I said so," she replied. "If you will all be quiet, I will sing a song for you."

The troll mama began to sing, "Ai-ai-ai-ai, boof, Ai-ai-ai-ai, boof, boof, Ai-ai-ai-ai, boof."

Soon, all her troll children were asleep. The troll mama tiptoed outside the cave to sit down with her sewing. She had not been there long before she heard a crying from the valley below.

"It sounds like human children," she thought. That was strange, for trolls live far away from humans. Trolls did not like people and people feared trolls. There were many stories of trolls eating humans. They were not true, of course, but most humans believed them.

The troll mama left the entrance to the cave and followed the sound. It did not take her long to find the children. Two small girls were huddled together under a big fir tree. They looked so miserable and scared that the troll mama felt sorry for them.

"Why are you here?" she asked gently.

"We . . . we . . . lost our way when we went to pick blueberries," they both sobbed.

"I will take you home with me," the troll mama said. "You must be hungry and cold. Tomorrow I will see what I can do to get you home."

A troll can be as big as a house or human-sized. They have big noses and big ears, hands, and feet. They also have tails. Some trolls have only one eye. Most trolls live in caves in the woods or mountains of Norway. Some are kind and nice, while others are angry and nasty. I almost saw one myself one summer when I was ten years old and picking berries in the high mountains of Norway.

The children were still frightened, but the troll did seem kind. She lifted the girls up and carried them to the cave. She fed them some bread, cheese, and milk, then tucked them into bed with the troll children.

Soon, the girls were sleeping peacefully. They were still sleeping when the littlest troll woke up.

"Mama, Mama!" he yelled. "Who is that in our bed? They look like trolls, almost, but their noses and ears are smaller and they have no tails!"

"No tails?" the other troll children echoed. "How strange! Everybody has tails! Foxes, bears, mice, squirrels, everybody!"

"Maybe somebody cut their tails off," said the littlest troll.

All of this loud talk woke up the girls. They looked around at the trolls and were scared.

"You don't have to be afraid of me," said the littlest troll. "I am nice and I would love to play with you."

When they heard this, the girls were no longer frightened. After a big breakfast, the older troll children had to help with chores around the cave while the girls and the youngest trolls went outside to play.

The girls had never had so much fun. They went mud sliding and tree climbing. They played hide-and-seek and tag. It was only when their stomachs began to growl that they found their way back to the cave.

The girls now looked more like trolls than like little girls. They had mud all over and twigs and leaves sticking out of their hair.

"I'd better take the two of you home," the troll mama exclaimed, laughing, "before you grow tails! I am sure your parents are very worried by now."

Early September is apple harvest time, and all the children love to help. They climb the trees to pick the apples nobody else can reach. After the good apples have been carefully picked, the children shake the trees to send the rest of the apples raining down on each other.

The troll mama, her eleven children and the two girls set out to find the house where the girls lived. It was quite a long walk, and the littlest trolls grew tired.

"Carry me," they each demanded. The troll mama picked up the two youngest trolls and the girls, and that's how they arrived at the girls' house later that evening.

The girls' parents had quite a fright when they saw all of the trolls on the doorstep, but they quickly understood that the trolls meant no harm and had brought the girls home safely.

The girls' father invited the trolls in for dinner. He got out his guitar and began singing to all of the children. Meanwhile, the troll mama and the girls' mother were in the kitchen preparing dinner. To the surprise of the girls' mother, the troll mama knew a lot about cooking. She taught the girls' mother how to make the best troll chicken.

After dinner, the girls' father said, "You know something? This is the best chicken

I have ever had. You trolls sure know how to cook."

The troll mama was very pleased by the father's comments and knew that the two families would be friends from this day forward.

"I am tired," the littlest troll whined. "I want my bed."

"Well, that's the first time I have ever heard you say that," the troll mama exclaimed. She turned to the little girls and their parents and said, "It's time for me to take my children home. Come and visit us next time you are in my neck of the woods."

Troll Chicken
— SERVES 8 —

YOU WILL NEED: a large roasting pan at least 3 inches deep, a lid or foil to cover the pan

2 chickens or
    1 chicken breast per person
1 can tomato paste
½ cup brown sugar
¼ cup oil

½ cup water
1 teaspoon ginger
½ teaspoon pepper
½ teaspoon salt
¼ cup soy sauce

1. Heat oven to 400 degrees.

2. Cut each chicken in half, and then cut off the legs from each half to make four pieces. Clean the pieces and place them in the roasting pan.

3. In a bowl, mix all the other ingredients together. Then pour the mixture over the chicken.

4. Cover the pan with the lid or put foil over the pan and tighten it all around. Put the pan in the oven.

5. Let the chicken bake in the oven for 1½ hours. Turn the pieces every half hour until they are done.

6. If you like your chicken crispy, place it on a grill for 5 minutes on each side; otherwise eat it as is.

7. Serve with rice and a salad.

The Nasty Witch

HELEN WAS NOT A NICE WITCH on any day of the year. This morning, she woke up in a particularly nasty mood. She tried to kick the dog as she got out of bed, but missed and stubbed her toe instead.

Then, with one of her spells, the witch changed the dog into a chicken. The poor dog hoped the spell would wear off before too long or he would have to see the wizard again. He hated being a chicken. Helen had turned him into a chicken before.

The bad witch was a big problem for the people on the farms nearby. When they saw her coming, they hid in fear. She had turned children into stone and cows into mice. No one knew what she would do next.

The dog hobbled up the mountain to where the wizard lived and pecked at the door with his chicken's beak.

"You poor dog!" the wizard exclaimed. "The witch has turned you into a chicken again." With a snap of his fingers, the dog was once again a dog.

The wizard was helpful and always tried to undo the wrongdoings of the witch. But he was getting tired of undoing her spells. He was too busy inventing his own new creations. Last year, he had invented colors. The world had been a very gray and boring place before that.

Just that morning, he had finished the potion that would make the witch disappear forever. Maybe now, he could have some peace and quiet. The potion had not been easy to make. The recipe for witch repellent in his spell book had been partially destroyed, and he had spent the last seven days experimenting to get it right.

The wizard's biggest problem would be to get the witch to take the potion. She was always so disagreeable.

"She's also greedy," the wizard thought. "I'm going to trick her somehow."

The wizard decided to have a party and not invite the witch. She would then be sure to come and make trouble.

He sent a messenger to town to invite all the townspeople. The magician waved his magic wand and made ice cream, cakes, candies, chocolates, cookies, and delicious cream puffs. Last, he made the punch he hoped would get rid of the witch.

In a big saucepan, the wizard started to mix the ingredients together. Then, from a green bottle, he added four spoonfuls of witch repellent. (Witch repellent is hard to find. If you ever need any, ask the wizard who lives nearest to you. Most wizards can make up a batch.)

The wizard tasted the punch and was satisfied. The repellent would work its spell only on the witch and was quite harmless to anyone else.

By dinnertime, all of the wizard's guests had arrived. His house was filled with happy, laughing people. It was not long before a big crash was heard outside. The witch had never mastered graceful landings on her broom. She always crashed.

The witch flung the door open and entered the room.

"Ha, ha!" she cackled. "So you think you're having a good time, eh? I am hungry and thirsty and I will eat everything here. Nothing will be left for you. Then, I will turn you all into bugs!"

The village people were not as afraid of the witch now that the wizard was there, but they were still worried.

The witch gobbled up all of the cakes, candies, and other goodies. When she had eaten every crumb, she picked up the punch bowl and drank it dry. All of a sudden, the witch turned bright red. In a puff of black smoke, she was gone.

"Back to the party!" the magician said. "Now we have a reason to celebrate."

Again he swung his magic wand and ice cream, cakes, cookies, and candies appeared for everyone to enjoy. The wizard and the villagers danced and ate until the sun came up.

The villagers were not the only ones who rejoiced. Outside, they could hear the dog howling for joy.

As for the witch, she was never seen again.

October is often a very stormy month with icy weather. The sea is very rough, and the waves are huge. Beaches are left littered with the debris of fall storms.

Magician's Brew
— Makes 20 Servings —

You will need: a large saucepan for cooking, a punch bowl, a knife for cutting the fruit, a juicer

2 cups water
2 cups sugar
1 quart strawberries
¾ cup canned of fresh pineapple
1 cup mixed fresh fruit (apples, grapes, oranges, apricots, etc.)

juice of 3 oranges
juice of 2 lemons
1 quart carbonated water
4 cups crushed ice or ice cubes
1 banana, sliced

1. Place the water and sugar in the saucepan.

2. Put the saucepan on the stove and turn the heat up. When the water and sugar begin to boil, turn the heat down and let the liquid simmer for 5 minutes.

3. Turn off the heat and allow the sugar and water to cool.

4. Rinse the strawberries in cold water and snip the green stems off with a knife. Cut the strawberries in half.

5. Cut the other fruit into small pieces.

6. Pour the sugar-water mixture into a punch bowl and add the fruit and the juices of the lemons and oranges.

7. Just before you are ready to serve the punch, stir in the carbonated water and the ice.

8. Slice the banana and put it in last.

9. Serve.

November

The Big Purple Spider

VERONICA, WHO THOUGHT SHE WAS a big purple spider, had to take her pretend web down. Her babysitter had told her to clean up.

"Spiders spin webs," she grumbled. "They don't take them down."

"Well, you are not a spider," the babysitter had replied, "only a girl with a spidery imagination. Now, clean this mess up before I trip on the strings."

"It would be fun to be a real spider," Veronica thought to herself. "I would creep up the babysitter's neck and really scare her. Then, maybe she would run out of the house screaming and never come back. No, that would not be nice. She is not that bad."

Veronica opened the hallway closet, then turned around to see if the chest of drawers were opening. Yes, it worked. She had attached strings to almost everything with a knob or handle on it. So, when the front door swung open and the babysitter's boyfriend came in, the oven door opened at the same time.

"Rad," the babysitter's boyfriend exclaimed as he removed his muddy boots by the front door. "You are really something, kid."

"I am not a kid. I am a spider," Veronica said.

"Okay, spider. My name is Robert, or Weird Robert, as they call me at the bakery where I work."

"You make cakes all day? Yummy! Would you make a cake for me?" Veronica asked.

"As it happens," Weird Robert replied, "I have come to take over. The changing of the guard, so to speak. Your babysitter has to go to the dentist."

Veronica and Weird Robert stepped aside as the babysitter, in a flurry of scarves and handbags, stormed out of the door.

"Let's get busy, kiddo," Weird Robert said as he made his way into the kitchen. "What do I call you?"

"Just call me the purple spider," Veronica said.

"What kind of cake should we make today, purple spider?" Weird Robert asked.

"Or, is that a stupid question? Bug cakes, of course."

"This purple spider's favorite food today is bug cupcakes," Veronica decided.

After they had taken everything they needed to make cupcakes out of the cupboard, Weird Robert mixed the batter in a big bowl. "This should be enough to feed a roomful of spiders. Okay, purple spider, where are the muffin tins and the paper cups?"

They filled the paper cups with batter and put the muffin tins in the oven. When the bug cakes smelled ready, Weird Robert and the big purple spider peeked into the oven.

"Just right," Weird Robert said. "They are light brown on top."

While the cupcakes were cooling, Weird Robert and the big purple spider mixed six different colored frostings. Weird Robert had also found some sprinkles, a few candies left over from a birthday party, raisins, nuts, and some marshmallows.

"First, we spread the frosting over the top and then we make the cupcakes into bugcakes with the decorations," Weird Robert said.

The big purple spider made two flies, six ladybugs, and many beetles. Weird Robert made many different beetles and a few imaginary bugs. He got out two big glasses of milk and sat down with Veronica to eat a few of the bugs.

The big purple spider managed to eat three and Weird Robert ate at least five. That was when the big purple spider's mom walked in and looked as if she were going to faint on the spot.

"They're not real bugs," Veronica, the big purple spider, said. "Don't worry."

"It's not that," her mom said. "But, what a mess! I am not putting another foot in this kitchen until it's cleaned up. I feel exhausted just looking at this house. And, why is there string everywhere?"

"I am a purple spider," Veronica said, "and spiders spin webs, of course."

"Of course," her mom replied. She grabbed a pair of scissors and left Veronica and Weird Robert to clean up the kitchen while she attacked the webs.

"All good things must come to an end," Weird Robert said, "so let's clean up. It's not as bad as it looks."

It took Weird Robert and Veronica only a short time to clean up. Spiders and Weird Roberts can sure get the job done when they have a few tasty bug cupcakes in their stomachs.

The lakes and ponds freeze over at the beginning of November, and by the end of the month they are thick, still, and glassy—perfect for ice skating. Children enjoy winter activities like ice skating, skiing, and having snowball fights.

Bug Cupcakes

— Makes 21 Cupcakes —

You will need: a mixing bowl, paper cupcake cups, muffin tin

1 stick of butter
1 cup sugar
3 teaspoons lemon juice
   (2 teaspoons vanilla and
   3 teaspoons cocoa powder,
   if you want to make
   chocolate cupcakes)
4 eggs
1 cup sour cream
3 cups flour

1 teaspoon baking powder
1 teaspoon baking soda

Icing and decorations:
3 cups powdered sugar
2 teaspoons lemon juice
2 egg whites
food coloring
M&Ms, candies, raisins, nuts, candy
   sprinkles, and marshmallows

1. Heat oven to 350 degrees.

2. Put the butter and sugar into the mixing bowl and beat until fluffy. Add the lemon juice, eggs, and sour cream, then beat some more.

3. Mix in the rest of the cupcake ingredients and stir the batter until everything is well blended.

4. Put the paper cups into the muffin tin and fill each cupcake paper three-quarters full with batter.

5. Put the muffin tin into the oven for about 15 minutes, or until the cupcakes are light brown on top.

6. Let the cupcakes cool completely before you decorate them.

Icing:

1. Pour 3 cups powdered sugar and lemon juice into a small bowl. If the icing is too thick, add some water, a few drops at a time while you stir.

2. Put the icing into 3 or more cups and mix different colored food coloring into each one.

3. Decorate as you please, but if you use candies or sprinkles, put them on right away before the icing dries.

The Nisse's Christmas

IT WAS THE DAY BEFORE CHRISTMAS EVE. The little old nisse *(pronounced NISS-eh)* was so sad. As he petted the barn cat, he told her, "Nobody will remember me this Christmas, either. Before, in my younger days, there was always somebody who remembered and believed in me and brought me rice porridge for Christmas. Maybe they have forgotten how to make it altogether." To get rice porridge on Christmas Eve was as important to the nisse as presents are to you and me on our birthdays.

The old nisse lived in the barn. He made sure that the animals were healthy and safe. Nisses are very shy and rarely seen by people. People today, the nisse thought, only believe in what they can see.

The cat listened to the nisse's sad story. The cat cared for the nisse and wanted to help him. When the nisse went to sleep the following morning, for nisses sleep mostly during the daytime, the cat went to see the little girl who lived on the farm. She was the only one who could understand cat language.

"Kjersti, put down your knitting and follow me," the cat told the girl.

Kjersti followed him to the barn. Behind the hay in the far corner, she saw something red sticking up out of the pile.

"Pull back the hay," the cat whispered, "and wake the nisse."

"A nisse?" Kjersti asked. "I have heard of nisses, but I've never seen one."

Gently, she shook the nisse awake. He sat up and rubbed his eyes.

"But it's still daytime," he grumbled. "Why are you waking me?"

"The cat told me it was important," Kjersti answered.

The nisse then told Kjersti why he was so miserable and sad. He told her all about Christmas customs nobody seemed to remember anymore, like making rice porridge

---

The nisse is short, has a long white beard, and wears a red hat with a pom-pom on the tip, a blue or white shirt, a red vest and socks, and blue mittens. He wears leather boots or clogs on his feet. The nisse lives in a stable or barn and protects and cares for the animals.

for the nisse and the children on Christmas Eve, heart baskets for the Christmas tree, and jule nek for the birds. "There are so many things that no one remembers anymore," he sighed. "If you would like to learn about these things, I will teach you. But we don't have much time. It's almost Christmas."

The next day, long before daylight, when everyone else was asleep, the nisse and the girl got busy in the kitchen. The nisse built a fire in the stove while Kjersti got out a large pot for the porridge.

"Take ten cups of milk and five cups of rice and pour them into the pot," the nisse explained. "Then add a pinch of salt and three spoonfuls of sugar. Bring it to a slow boil but make sure that it doesn't burn. When the milk starts to boil, turn the fire low and let it simmer. But keep an eye on it," the nisse said.

Kjersti did as she was told and, soon, she had a sweet-smelling porridge.

"Take the porridge off the stove and put a lid on it. Let it sit while we make heart baskets for the Christmas tree. Here, let's see what I have. I have gold, red, yellow, green, and blue paper, glue, and scissors. It's easy. Just fold the paper like this," the nisse explained. "Cut two half hearts and weave them together. Then, cut a small strip of paper and glue a handle on the basket." *(Directions on page 50.)*

"Oh, they are so pretty!" Kjersti exclaimed. "Let's make a lot of them and hang them on the tree!"

And so they did.

The nisse was in such a happy mood. He sang all the Christmas carols he knew. Some of them he had to sing two or three times so that Kjersti could learn them, too.

"I think the rice porridge is just right. We should have a taste just to make sure."

The nisse got out three bowls: one for Kjersti, one for the cat, and one for himself.

Kjersti dished the porridge into the bowls, and the nisse sprinkled sugar and cinnamon on top. In the middle, he put a spoonful of butter.

"This is yummy," Kjersti said. "I don't know why my mother has never made this."

"Maybe she has forgotten how," the nisse said.

On December 13th, Scandinavians celebrate Santa Lucia Day, the official start of the Christmas season. Young girls dress in white gowns and tie red sashes around their waists. On their heads, they wear wreathes decorated with white candles. The purposes of this tradition are to bring light into a dark month and ward off evil.

"But now you can teach her and, when you are older, you can teach your children, too. Let's clean up here and go to the barn to get straw to make nek for the birds. The poor birds!" the nisse said. "Sometimes there is too much snow and they can't find anything to eat. To make nek is easy," he continued. "Just gather an armful of straw that has seed on top and tie a rope tightly around it. Then, put a long stick into the middle and plant it in the snow outside. Now, the birds will have food for Christmas, too."

The nisse had grown tired and needed a nap.

"I'm so glad I met you," Kjersti said. "I want to be your friend forever."

"That would make me very happy," he replied.

Kjersti went inside to wake up her family. "You won't believe what happened," Kjersti told her mother. "I met a nisse and he has shown me how to make all kinds of things."

"That's nice," her mother replied. She did not believe her. But, when she saw with her own eyes what Kjersti and the nisse had made, she had to wonder if nisses really did exist after all.

Jule Porridge
— Makes 10 servings —

YOU WILL NEED: a large saucepan, a wooden spoon

5 cups short grain rice
10 cups milk
½ teaspoon salt
3 tablespoons sugar

1 teaspoon vanilla
butter
cinnamon
sugar

1. Pour the milk, rice, salt, sugar, and vanilla into the saucepan and stir it all together.

2. Put the pot on the stove and turn the heat on, but not too hot (medium). Bring the porridge to a boil, then turn the heat to low and let it simmer for an hour or so. Make sure you keep an eye on it so it doesn't burn or boil over.

3. When the rice grain has evened out, the porridge is done. If the porridge is too thick, you can add more milk.

4. Pour the porridge into individual bowls, put a teaspoonful of butter in the middle, then sprinkle cinammon and sugar on top. Cranberry juice is good to drink with rice porridge.

CHRISTIN FJELD DRAKE grew up in Oslo, Norway, where she heard folktales of trolls, fairies, wolves, princes, princesses, and other creatures that were meant to enliven the imagination, give a bit of advice, tell a piece of history, or teach a skill. She now resides in Flagstaff, Arizona, where she once had an acclaimed restaurant called The Lost Norwegian, which inspired a gorgeous cookbook of the same name. Now a preschool teacher, the author hopes her tales will inspire a new generation of children to be creative in the kitchen and visualize their own stories.

ALEXANDRA ELDRIDGE is a painter, designer, illustrator, instructor, and artistic director who graduated Summa Cum Laude with a Bachelor of Arts from Ohio University and went on to complete an honors thesis at Cambridge University. Her art has been displayed in exhibitions in Ohio, New York, New Jersey, Vermont, and in her home town of Santa Fe, New Mexico, where she lives with her two sons, Saxon and Sebastian.

HOW TO MAKE HEART BASKETS

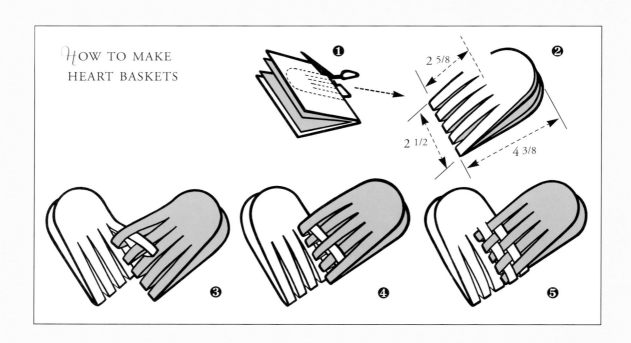